*HERE THERE WAS
ONCE A COUNTRY*

HERE THERE WAS ONCE A COUNTRY

Vénus Khoury-Ghata

*Translated from the French
by Marilyn Hacker*

OBERLIN COLLEGE PRESS
Oberlin, Ohio

www.oberlin.edu/~ocpress

*Cet ouvrage, publié dans le cadre d'un programme d'aide à la publica-
tion, bénéficie du soutien du Ministère des Affaires étrangères et du Ser-
vice Culturel de l'Ambassade de France aux Etats-Unis.* This work,
published as part of a program of aid for publication, received sup-
port from the French Ministry of Foreign Affairs and the Cultural
Services of the French Embassy in the United States.

Library of Congress Cataloging-in-Publication Data

Khoury-Ghata, Vénus (translations and introduction by Marilyn
Hacker)
    Here There Was Once a Country
    (The FIELD Translation Series v. 25)
    I. Title. II. Series.

LC: 2001088570
ISBN: 0-932440-89-4 (pbk.)

CONTENTS

Translator's Preface   vii

Widow   1

The Dead Man's Monologue   5

The Seven Honeysuckle Sprigs of Wisdom   29

Early Childhood   51

TRANSLATOR'S PREFACE

Vénus Khoury-Ghata was born in Lebanon in December, 1937; she has lived in France since 1972. Not the child of the intelligentsia or the diplomatic world like many literary émigrés, she was born to a Maronite Christian family, one of four children of a village police-man and a housewife she's described as "illiterate in two languages." It was the poet's younger brother who first aspired to a literary ca-reer; it was also her brother who was the tyrannical father's scape-goat, who turned to drugs in his teens and was paternally immured in a rudimentary mental hospital. This marking story was recounted lyrically by Khoury-Ghata in 1998 in *Une maison au bord des larmes* (*A House on the Edge of Tears*)—the only one of her fourteen novels which eschews fictional invention for autobiographical material. This novel shares the counterpoint present in all of Khoury-Ghata's poetry, between the immediate lyric or narrative and the backdrop of contemporary history—the history of war-torn Lebanon. In the construction of the poet's personal myth of origins, it was the silenc-ing of the gifted, vulnerable brother which gave his sister access to the written word. (In the same year that Khoury-Ghata published *Une maison au bord des larmes,* her sister, the journalist May Mé-nassa, who stayed in Lebanon and writes in Arabic, published a novel on the same subject—neither sister knew of the other's project before the books appeared.)

Khoury-Ghata's work bridges the anti-lyrical surrealist tradition which has informed modern French poetry since Baudelaire and the parabolic and communal narrative with its (we might say Homeric) repetitions of metaphors and semi-mythic tropes of Arabic poetry. Though there are many Francophone poets of Arab origin, including women poets such as Andrée Chedid, Joyce Mansour and Nadia Tueni, Khoury-Ghata's work is unique in its synthesis of the quotidian and the fantastic, its conciliation of the narrative and the lyric. She is the author of nine books of poems, most of which have for implicit backdrop the language and landscape of the poet's mother country. Though she was raised bilingual, her mother tongue was Arabic, and her earliest writings were in that language. She writes: "Nourished by the two languages, I write in Arabic through the French language—when my poems are translated into Arabic, they seem to be returning to their original language. For years, my first drafts were written in both languages, the Arabic going from right to left on the page and the French from left to right: they crossed each other's paths in the middle. Twenty-eight years in Paris haven't cured me of my mother tongue: when there's a problem, I take refuge in it, and am surprised when the people with whom I'm speaking don't understand!"

As she oscillates between French and Arabic, Khoury-Ghata moves with equal fluidity between poetry and fiction, and, in her poems especially, between life and death. Death becomes another mode of life, an ironic one carried on six feet below our surfaces, where the dead, according to the poet's own mythology, and once more not unlike Homeric shades, "nourish themselves on the smell of our bread, drink the steam rising from our water, live on our noises." Death itself has a double register: as experienced on a personal level, but with the collective specter of 200,000 people dead in Lebanon during the war that marked the poet's youth serving as a chorus in the intimate tragedy. The personal mourning informing the "Dead Man's Monologue" is for Jean Ghata, the poet's second husband, research physician and father of the youngest of her four children. But the "dead man" (who, in fact, does not speak a monologue, but is described "living out his death") ceases to be an individual with a history. He's not the man of science, the beloved spouse, a tutelary spirit in some existence beyond this one; he is Everyman in the oddly circumscribed "village" of death, neither Elysian Fields nor bustling necropolis but local and self-regarding—in fact, like the Lebanese villages of "The Seven Honeysuckle Sprigs of Wisdom" and "Early Childhood."

According to Khoury-Ghata, the word "death" is a cornerstone of her work, making its way into several titles. This began for her "in 1975 with the unbearable images of Lebanon drowned in its own blood. Cadavers were laid out on wooden planks to be shoved into ditches for common burial with the same movement as a baker putting bread into the oven." Death: daily bread for the Lebanese. "I felt guilty about transforming the dead into words, lining them up like lead soldiers on my pages, but I was incapable of turning to another subject. Five years later, this collective death gave way to an individual death, that of my husband, the father of my daughter. Death which I'd picked up and examined barehanded blew up in my face...."

Khoury-Ghata wrote a wrenching book of poems, *Un faux pas du soleil* (*A Misstep of the Sun*), while her husband was dying, "imploring him to live, not to cross that irremovable barrier, attaching him to his favorite objects, to his books, like a goat tethered to a stake...but death had the last word. It worked over my life like a meager field with its implacable harrow...." She turned toward fiction after that, and it was only with the alleviation of her mourning that she came back to poetry and wrote "The Dead Man's Monologue," which touches the same subject. Though this elegy is touched with humor, with a quality of fable, she still wrote it "as you'd dig a ditch, with huge shovelfuls of sentences that dropped with a noise like falling earth: I was digging a written grave."

The reference to a Thou who may be at once a God and a human beloved (an avatar of love) which one finds in Rumi, in

Hafiz, in Ghalib, is absent from Khoury-Ghata's poetry, marked though it is by Arabic and even Persian poetic traditions. The *mythologos* here is of humanity, a meta-humanity at once more circumscribed and larger than life. In the village of Khoury-Ghata's poems, angels may converse with sign-painters and a pomegranate tree hang about a housewife's back door like a recalcitrant child. But just as Moslems, Christians and Jews unhierarchically cohabit the village of "The Seven Honeysuckle Sprigs of Wisdom," neither the angelic nor the vegetable orders seem more powerful or prescient than the modest mother who, in "Early Childhood," puts the stars, clouds and seasons in order. There is markedly no God in "The Dead Man's Monologue"—the dead have no more of an insider's view of the universe's workings than the living. Indeed, in "The Seven Honeysuckle Sprigs of Wisdom," the dead co-exist and cohabit with the living. The village cemetery is more or less the wrong side of town, a barrio of the ultimately disenfranchised, who triple up in their graves in hard times, and can disparage no one: the dead could only look down on someone more dead than themselves.

Much of Khoury-Ghata's poetry, as well as *Une maison au bord des larmes*, could be described by Audre Lorde's term "biomythography," which Lorde coined for her own narrative *Zami*. Lorde's book resembles the classical memoir/*bildungsroman* more closely than does anything in Khoury-Ghata's work. What they have in common is at once their ex-centricity: the West Indian child in the Bronx, the Lebanese writer in Paris, and the enracination of their texts in an historical macrocosm which is rarely specified and everywhere implied: in Khoury-Ghata's case, the war in Lebanon, the state of siege in her mother country that is everywhere reflected in her work, presaged in the texts going back to a time preceding it, which was the time of her childhood and adolescence. An American reader wonders—is there as much rage collecting behind the seeming bemused and ironic resignation in Khoury-Ghata's enigmatic fables as there is in Lorde's parables? Given her country's recent history, how can there not be? Yet it is nowhere made evident in the poems: rather, it aliments them with a condensed energy which is "furious" in the sense of the word's etymology: it illumines them from within with a contained, volcanic fire.

While Lorde's "biomythography" has an autobiographical focus shared by her poems, in Khoury-Ghata's poems the "I," any speaker or figure, first-person singular or otherwise, whom the reader can interpret as standing for the poet herself, is a "significant absence" (as Mallarmé called Rimbaud); this is certainly true in the three sequences collected here. The enigmatic "she" of the poem I've taken the liberty of entitling "Widow" (a poem untitled in French; the sequences keep their original titles) is as close as we come. The point of view of the initially "familial" sequence, "Early Childhood," is a "we," which at first seems to be the cohort of siblings but which expands itself to include (possibly) the children of an entire culture, or children in general, bemused and half-wild, bewildered and yet more in touch with the agonized universe in all its manifestations than their elders. (Several of the poems are dedicated to May Ménassa, the writer/journalist sister who shared Khoury-Ghata's real childhood.) But the numinous protagonist of "Early Childhood" is a mother who partakes at once of the terrestrial, angelic and chthonic orders, who assumes herself on speaking terms with God and an assortment of angels. She ventures no further in her waking life than the cast shadow of a dining-room's lampshade, but wanders to the ends of the universe in her sleep. She has daily commerce with the dead, and if she has a lover, it is a poet she mistrusts deeply who has been defunct for a hundred years: is the child she fears he will engender her poet daughter, her daughter's poems? How unexpectedly and deftly, though, the sequence's focus changes as it nears its end, exchanging the first-person plural of the children for a "they" who have colonized the country, made pornographic usage of its trees, imposed a multicolored but alien language.

"The Seven Honeysuckle Sprigs of Wisdom" is the most recent

sequence in the book, written in 1998. Though not devoid of ominous shadows, it seems an almost Arcadian *Cahier d'un retour au pays natal*, to a village which may or may not ever have existed. Religion is gently mocked from the opening (the priest has gone off in pursuit of a crow who cawed in biblical Aramaic), but the co-existence of Christians, Moslems and Jews is taken for granted. Authority is mocked as well, though we cannot but admire the conscientious schoolmaster who tries out the letters of the Arabic alphabet for practical use before imposing them on the children. The trees speak Arabic too, and may not answer to their names in French. Khoury-Ghata describes this sequence as her fantasia on a venerable rural Arab tradition of public story-telling about the neighbors, inventing and embroidering more and more outrageous (and poetic) lies. We remember Zora Neale Hurston's Florida front-porch storytellers—but the composition in *patois* of slightly scandalous oral poems about the butcher's doings with the baker's wife and the priest's pheasant-poaching was also a savory feature of village life in France up through the first half of the 20th century. Khoury-Ghata has used this probably-universal proto-fictional pastime to create a poet's vision of sources—not individual this time, but collective, with diverse names, ages, genders, a source as multifaceted and bilingual as the poet herself.

Marilyn Hacker
Paris, 2001

WIDOW

WIDOW

The first day after his death
she folded up her mirrors
put a slipcover on the spider web
then tied up the bed which was flapping its wings to take off.

The second day after his death
she filled up her pockets with wood chips
threw salt over the shoulder of her house
and went off with a tree under each arm.

The third day after his death
she swore at the pigeons lined up along her tears
bit into a grape which scattered its down in her throat
then called out till sunset to the man gone barefoot
into the summer pasture in the cloudy mountains.

The fourth day
a herd of buffalo barged into her bedroom
demanding the hunter who spoke their dialect
she shouldered her cry
shot off a round
which pierced the ceiling of her sleep.

The fifth day
shoe-soles of blood imprinted themselves on her doorstep
she followed them to that ditch where everything smells of boned
    hare.

3

The sixth day after his death
she painted her face with earth
attacked the peaceful shadows of passers-by
slit the throats of trees
their colorless blood evaporated when it touched her hands.

The seventh day
stringy men sprouted in her garden
she mistook them for poplars
bit the armpits of their branches
and lengthily vomited wood-chips.

The eighth day
the sea whinnied at her door
she washed her belly's embankments
then called down to the river's mouth
where men clashed together like pebbles.

The ninth day
she dried her tears on the roof between the basil and the budding
    fog
gazed at herself in stones
found cracks in her eyes like those in a church's stained glass.

The tenth day
he surged up out of her palm
sat down on her fingernail
demanded her usual words to drink and the almond odor of her
    knees
He swallowed them without pleasure
on his journey he'd lost the taste for tortured water.

THE DEAD MAN'S MONOLOGUE

You say when you happen to die
the darkness is only frightening at night
when the fearful dead hold their black breath.

THEY

They float on the surface of memory
seep into the walls with the moon's phases
slit water's throat
dismantle the clocks.

They clamber up roots
hurtle down the slope of rain
breathe in the steam rising from wells
drink our flooding rivers in one gulp.

They straddle rooftops
bend the beams
wake the children curled up in their lashes
to make them listen to their finger-joints cracking.

They eat the flesh of the jujube tree
tie up the arms of the cypress
and use it as a candle.

They fly through the air above cemeteries
knock down the tombstones
empty their contents in the gutters.

They snow down in motionless flakes
breathe out inert gusts
we gather them on the ledge of our hips
steep them in our sweat
wring out their tears
dry them on underground clotheslines.

They harness our nights
saddle our dreams
mount us from the heart's forgetful side.

They come between the walnut tree and its bark
force open the doors of November
pierce the skylight's eye
sign our mirrors with their steam.

They retreat into their bodies
go to ground in their ankles
cry up to the groin
so industrious these dead when they crawl beneath the plains
to gather nuts the summer rejected
and shake them like a baby's rattle.

We were
often awakened by the odor of their smoke
chilly combustions that opposing winds turned into ice.

We live standing on their silence
erect on their rectilinear shadow
we trample them by day
they pace across us at night
the foliage of their footsteps whips our nostrils.

They borrow all our orifices
cross our underground waters
navigate our arteries at low flesh-tide
avoiding the iliac shores.

They push apart our under-wings
grab our feathers
lap up the salt from our crests
soil us with a cry.

They clear the underbrush from beneath the plains
grate up hemp from the hillocks
lap up the pond's overflow
then go away drunk on our liquor.

They undo the maze of blood and road
dig furrows for belly and vine
swing in violent tremors between our ribs
migrate from foreheads to plateaus
break down partitions between soil and soil
their passage provokes a vertical flight of insects
all that remains of them once they've passed through earth's
     swinging door.

They inundate us in our crevices and hollows
we dry them out at earth's low tide
They empty us of our embraces
we fill them up with our strides
They install themselves in our corners
bloat the darkness
They think they are indispensable to the motion of swamps.

They stretch out as far as the moon
we bend them down to the underground passageways
chase them away from our houses
make them lose their way by changing the country's slope
and the way it faces the light.

They swell until they fill the sources
install themselves in bread-boxes and bells
mount noon from the still side of the clock.

They possess the planet completely.

He comes back
a flintstone's shadow
reflection of a banished image
without being invited into her earthly skin
He forces the birch tree's lock
bends back the guardrail's fingers
demands her equatorial sweat and her sorrow to drink

"Your tears are glass and your anguish is paper"
he cries, surging up from a fissure of her blood
She wonders if she should keep him there
dress him in his body hung behind the doors

She calls him until sunset
emphasizing the first syllable of his name
which she offers to feed passers-by who've asked her for nothing.

He lacks nothing behind his wall of ice
the inverted tree eats its own leaves
and the linear path ends at his feet

He rehearses his body
He carries it like a candle
the wick of its gaze turned inwards

The long-traveled springs borrow his eyes
to put out his heart flaming in its salt

Stripped of his footsteps for having crossed the border of the
    world.

He collects the noises distilled by his walls
decants them to capture their contours
locks them with a double cry

His interlocutors
are an inverted beech and that cock-crow which pierces daylight
      three levels up
counting time backwards protects his fingers from the rust
which devours the steps of the evaporated ladder

Unable to say where he broke off his relations with roads
from now on his folded feet pace up and down a nonexistent
      space.

14

He shovels huge mounds of thick air from the depths
then stacks it in blocks around his absent body

Stains spread out on the narrow surface of day
he gauges his heart by how much cold it holds
his mouth by its content of chalk
and hews cornerstones for his hips

His longing for speech makes him scratch at the ground in search
    of words
his lips emit only splinters
since his house was darkened by a swallow's passage.

Sometimes
at a turning in the ashes
an extinguished stone lights up at the site of his house

Finding the windows lined up the same way again
eases his steps

His mouth full of darkness
he paces up and down his garden's underside keeping close to the
    termite-nest walls

He has that way of dragging his soul like a dog he wants to drive
    away.

Cold is his only guide
an abolished substance his fragile envelope

He laughs to find himself so perforated
then weeps at the sight of day slipping under his door

He leaves his darknesses lit up until dawn
to light the way for travelers whose feet are tied

Attached to his square of ash
he surveys his own combustion
poking at the frost in his fire

Pretended calcination
sham home
false silhouette carved in a block of shadow

A carousel which idles
It happened at a curve in the planet's orbit.

He says that the air strangles itself flying over his one wall
that the watchtower sun pursues his evaporated body

More than once he demands the liberation of the cry
which marked the rupture between his waters and his bones
more than once he inscribed his signature on the cracked marble
    to certify that he WAS

Sometimes beneath his threshold
that unawaited river presents itself
Stormy guest who floods his sleep
and disrupts the order of his ribs arranged in a wreath

Somnambulant water which follows the selvage of darkness
between the muteness of the air
and the cock-crow which scatters daylight three levels higher.

His dwelling a place of frost which flames up at the touch of a
     sound
the cold grass is his one interlocutor
a distant cockscomb his one color

He set sail on waves of earth
his shout when he moored made the cypress tremble

Time for him is a dismantled clock
since they placed his body lower than the planet
and let his fire die of hunger.

Painless space
nettles established their black kingdom there
the only occupant of the premises has folded up his heart and put
    away his gestures

Sometimes
that white wind which pursues the fenceposts

Wind measured out by the ounce
parsimoniously distributed among corners rounded off by distress
which tortures the absent lock at fixed hours

House built on the alignment of ploughed fields
the man who patched its stones together has crumbled to bits in its
    rooms

The widow who rolls his body down the slope
is as acid as a fruit and is cracked like bread

Despair as high as a storm
the lowlands whose flesh she bites
send her back to the hilltop where a broom-bush is sobbing
She descends the slope at the rectilinear hour
to knead her dead man with yeast
and thrust him into the oven of her belly.

Must we give the dead subsidiary work?
A madman cried out as far as the lagoon
denouncing the rushed moon-cycles
the illegible nights
the ocean's grip

He showed off women's underwear from the high countries
	stitched with blood
accused the rains of stacking themselves like bricks
between the wheat and its shadow
between the bark and the sapwood
the madman cried out until the continent was extinguished.

He complains about the brambles gripping each other on his
    threshold
about the bony air obstructing his openings
about the desert which moves into his chest in the dry season
filling his cage with gray grass that insults the wind at regular
    intervals

And also
when day prunes away its superfluous lines
there is that dead man at his skylight
watching a grave trample a poppy's bones.

His inverted house is not expected to have offspring
the last arrivals were dropped there through a crack in the air

Gray crowd in evening's grayness
bony crowd in the rib-cage of the absent wind

They descended the ladder accompanied by a rose
then they ignored each other

They should have massed together in a cluster
and followed the ash strolling from mound to mound

They could have coupled
proliferated.

He arises from his slumber
breaks up the air blocking his floor with hatchet-blows
so he can watch the ascent of underground clouds

Prisoner of his perimeter of cold
and of the cock's crow as it eats the vegetal crest above him
he hesitates at following the bloodless poplars
embarking on the din of the streams

Even so, when a thrown stone hits its ear
his house whinnies in the bone-stripped day.

He speaks to his tools with humility
the bone which drills each yawning gap
clay to be a belly for him
roots he needs to hang out his laundry of flesh

Cut off from moon-cycles
on the margin of the swamp
only the murmur of the coal mines reaches him

Neither T-square nor plumb line to measure time's angle
and verify the darkness's verticality
no implements to heat up the surrounding cold
and serve him his portion of earth
no key to open up the stones
and let him cry on his house's shoulder.

Some of the dead
the outmoded ones who sprout up on roadsides
crushers of stone and evening
install themselves at the border of the visible
between dog and wolf
between moon and howling

They complain that there are too many drawers in the earth
ranged in the order in which their occupants were forgotten

The first to arrive claim a view of the coal mines
and proximity to an underground river

Separated by their silences
they stare at the slippage of ground on their doorsteps
fear is one of their four elements

Don't question them
forget what master they work for
words rot on their tongues
ever since their hearts evaporated.

Migration of ashes from one wall to the other
He threads himself into the stone's weave, shrugs off his shadow
He twists the air parked on his plot of earth
and hangs it like a braid of garlic from the ceiling
then goes back to sleep

He has no need to look out through his shutters
to see the city without houses
the forest without trees
and the sun shrunk down to a dot

Punctual in timelessness
he wakes up the clay
and teaches it the first movements of pulleys and wind

No danger of late arrivals
Newcomers announce themselves with three pickaxe blows
and with those cables which start the descent of a rose

Eternity takes no longer than a petal to begin.

THE SEVEN HONEYSUCKLE
SPRIGS OF WISDOM

My village has three waterfalls three churches but no priest
The last one went off after a crow that cawed in Aramaic

Time in my village is in such a hurry that women whelp litters in
   seven days no skimpier than the ones you'd see elsewhere

My village's river turns back toward its source to avoid flowing
   through the neighboring hamlet with its wealth of three cars
   and an embalmed saint which attracts pilgrims.

Mokhtar the shoemaker reads the upside-down newspaper
    protecting his head from the sun
Wahiba the beggar empties the carafe of communion wine into her
    false-bottomed trousers
Maryam the new widow mates with all the trees that pass by

It's thanks to the crying chick that the fox finds the hen
says this selfsame Maryam who's been shelling pebbles since her
    garden got angry with the peas
the season's prime gravel simmers in her stew-pot
a seven-tailed stream sleeps in her bed

My village is endowed with two cemeteries
one cemetery open to the sky for the summer
another for the winter so large the dead can stretch out with their
    legs spread like pharaohs.

In my village the sheep are so tall they graze on the bellies of
        clouds, chew in the violets' shadows while slandering Mansour
        the wool-carder

In the beginning was the egg repeats Rahil morning and night and
        she breaks her rooster's eggs on the ironsmith's anvil
Rahil who was a communist well before Lenin and Siberia won't
        judge anyone
since her son slept with her she-goat and then bought her three
        necklaces and a gold nose-ring

Sometimes silhouettes loom up on the highest hilltop
ibex or wolf it makes no difference
Rahil's ball of yarn dissolves and knits coats for anyone who's cold.

One day when it was night two monks came through my village
with their bell and their smoking censer
Who were they burying at such a late hour?
Only the poplars along the road could see into the open coffin

Youssouf the cemetery caretaker accuses the dead of being sloppy
they eat the saltpeter off the walls and don't sweep up the crumbs
Behind that fence says the selfsame Youssouf, no one is at his best
you'd need someone more dead than you are to have something to
    boast about

Philomena has stopped sleeping with every male who passes by
ever since Marzouk the painter gave her features to a stained-glass
    angel
she's afraid of rumpling her wings.

Philomena's thoughts are as narrow as her skirts
her soul as high as her heels which are tangled in timidity since she
    started knitting a vest for the ironmonger

Amine is so wealthy that seven different-colored salts stand in state
    on his table
The rainbow which has a place at his table plunges its fingers
    seven times in a row in his jars before making a brief
    appearance on his balcony to the applause of passers-by

Sometimes Jacob sees horses galloping on the roof of the
    synagogue while the moon mocks them with crude words
    from the Kabbala
"Thank God it's only a dream" he stammers as he falls back to sleep
Jacob's daughter who had the misfortune of dreaming the same
    dream was turned into a stew-pot
spices and smoke were stirred together in her eyes.

Mordecai the hairdresser has painted a devil on his door to ward
    off thieves
his left hand cuts hair in hiding from his right hand on the Sabbath
the knife gripped between his jaws
It's to cut into the bread of sorrow while curling the rabbi's hair

Mordecai is neither believer nor heretic but balsamic like the
    vinegar in which Rachel's duck simmers when she has her
    period

Rachel never closes her door for fear of wearing out the hinges and
    keeping happiness from entering her house
The milkman who's mad about her says she's so hairy that his
    donkey could graze in her armpits while he shot off his rifle
    and chewed on lupine blooms.

Roads which cross other people's dreams don't lead anywhere
says Massouda the wise woman while blowing into the stem of her
    narguileh
Her smoke-rings make the canary dizzy; he suspects the earth of
    speeding up its rotation to reach night more quickly, night
    which fades his mistress's beauty

Massouda's cards never lie
Three aces followed by three jacks mean a plague of locusts
A change of mayor is inevitable when three kings line up on the
    table
Massouda's counsels are listened to by the archbishop whose Mass
    she prompts by making her bench creak

Khalil who made a fortune selling hay buttons up his fly on his
    marble balcony within sight of his mare
She recognizes him by the odor of his sweat and by his whip
    which lashes the clouds during droughts to make them rain
    on his field.

This selfsame Khalid had his head plunged in a basin of water
    perfumed with orange-blossoms when the bombing made his
    house crash to the ground
He regained his balance on a flagstone without spilling a drop of
    water

Maroun has quit his job in the brickyard to set up shop as a liar
He lies in winter especially when the wind busy howling in the
    gullies can't contradict him
Maroun claims to have downed a dozen quail with a stone
and to have started a storm by pissing in the wind
He surprised everyone by taking off for America with his coffee-pot
leaving his wife on the kitchen wall, hanging from a nail

The beggar Rassoul's mouth waters till it drips at the sight of
    Laouza
her belly is a white loaf blessed by the archbishop
her navel a cherry pecked by blackbirds.

Laouza goes into town every month to have her back
    photographed
Pain cuts her in two ever since she fell from the cherry tree which
    grew more quickly than her ladder
Her ewe's milk has turned black since a lizard gave her the evil eye
    through the skylight

This selfsame Laouza's pot of gardenias doesn't cheer up her
    parakeets which come from India
and which only smile at the postman who should bring them news
    from their cousins in New Delhi

The miser Mantouf divides his chestnuts between his pigs and the
    Armenian saint beatified for political reasons
The latter swallows them without pleasure and then excretes them
    in the holy-water font wrapped in paper from Armenia.

The mayor forbids the goats to graze on the French alphabet
forbids the schoolchildren to sleep in their books before they clean
their ears
forbids the plane trees on the village square to sit down on their
own shade
which would risk exposing the fountain to sunstroke as it spurts
like a spendthrift
spreading slander in front of the children

Maha the shepherdess traveled thousands of miles to reach Ali's
dream
but he closed the door of his sleep in her face
Everything in its own time, he said
only darkness is permitted to wander around at night

This selfsame Mantouf has become even stingier since the devil
pissed in his bread-box
obliging his mice to eat the neighbor's flour
and his chickens to peck in the devil's den.

Mantouf was a schoolmaster before he inadvertently stepped over
     a toad
A wellspring of science and information
he spit knowledge right into the children's mouths
and paid the butcher with buttons he tore off his fly

Mantouf's wife has ears as tender as vine-leaves beneath the arbor
a neck as supple as a syringa leaf in the sun
A bottle of vinegar shares her bed since her husband started
     sleeping with the stream
He comes home at dawn
his two fists clenched on his chest turned into pebbles

The legs of this selfsame Mantouf have grown shorter since his wife
     washed his pants
With the extra fabric she made three vests a pair of trousers and a
     bow-tie for the parish beggar.

When the priest the rabbi and the imam were invited to the poor
    man's table
they brought him three tufts of their beards which he planted in
    his garden
The three upside-down trees which grew nine months later
cast their shade on the devil's house

The schoolmaster Farhoud is so conscientious that he tries the
    alphabet out on himself before using it on the children
The letter Aleph is unreliable
its back is so fragile not even a hair could ride on it
"Mim" is a pious she-camel listening to the muezzin
"Ba" prefers jam to the dictionary
"Sin" is a coffee-pot with a pierced ear
"Zah's" axles creak since "tah" crushed its toe
"Tah" must be learned lying down standing up is bad for him

Farhoud lived in geography for a long time before moving into
    grammar
Asia Minor he says is only Asia Major's younger sister
and the poles an invention of a bear with a bad idea.

Farhoud can argue both sides of every question
in favor of the beggar on the square, promising him that after he
    dies he'll eat partridges at every meal
against his neighbor, saying that other people's bread doesn't fill
   your belly

Before he had a book Farhoud had a wife
whom he leafed through every morning in the direction of the
    sheets
from left to right as one speaks French
in the direction of the wind like Dutch windmills

Farhoud adopted three orphans with one month's salary
three raccoons who foraged from garbage cans in Montreal.

Monsieur Antoun sleeps in his tarboosh to show his scorn of the
    French colonists
From far off you'd take him for a poppy with just one petal
He earned the medals which cluster on his pajama-jacket
he emerged victorious from a battle with a whole hive of bees after
    he rubbed the drone's nose

Antoun's wife isn't the same since a pigeon shat on her head
she makes eyes at the stained-glass saint
and asks the stream to light her cigarette

Antoun's sister Khaoula has marmoreal thighs
volcanic breasts
and the crotch of a sergeant with hair as straight as matchsticks.

Khaoula didn't call the firemen when a fire broke out in her
    chicken-house
she put it out with her toothbrush-glass taking care not to wet the
    rooster's tailfeathers

The Christ in rags and tatters rummaging through the trashcan of
    Morcos the carpenter was looking for the fifth nail which once
    pierced his hip
The man who had walked in his death for two thousand years was
    chased to the church by dogs and bells; there he knelt before a
    taper which wept its wax on the feet of a crucified man

The selfsame Morcos was renowned for the comfort of his custom-
    made coffins
the pencil behind his ear dropped of its own accord to note the
    height of the deceased's sorrow and the area of the heart
    shrunk to the size of a walnut.

Magida the novice prostitute has willed her lamp to the luna
        moths, her inkwell to the fountain
her bed to the lark whose sex is shut
The bones found before her door were from the apple tree's
        skeleton
and jaws of the grass which squats in afflicted houses

Those who have seen Magida divide the winter into zones with her
        lamp
say that she holds it up high to chase away the fog
and pierce with its ray the frozen eyes of the partridge
and of God
whom she errs in calling by his nickname
not realizing he might get angry

The fate of Wahiba's plum tree is linked to the country's
        independence
Will it be the same translated into French
and will it answer to a name that perhaps won't suit its branches
        used to conversing with the Arab wind which postpones
        autumn for a month so it can inventory its leaves?

The schoolmaster Zakzouk is convinced that books have wings
which carry them high above the fountains
towards the twinkling alphabet of the stars which look like cumin
    seeds

Zakzouk who used to have his lectern beneath an olive tree
    abandoned arithmetic for singing exercise borrowed from the
    cricket

Two times donkey equals two
three times baaah equals goat
four times son equals nothing since the mayor's Ford ran down a
    flock of schoolboys.

The daily appearances of Saint Anthony in the well of Arbid the
    heretic provoke sarcasm from the clouds which double up
    with laughter when they see the halo floating on the water
and the priest blessing the crowd of cypresses as they fervently
    whip their own bark

Arbid's donkey is a direct descendant of Pythagoras
his deep thoughts inscribe themselves in tough meat on his shoes
Divided between hay and oats his customs declarations contain
    only losses
which make the sum fall over on its back

Mounir who made a fortune in cumin
says he's the cousin of the camel which flew from Zanzibar to
    Madagascar
leaving in a fold of the desert
a head of garlic
a clove
and the pit of a date once eaten by Mohammed.

Wahiba never crosses her legs for fear of tangling up her
    thoughts
The snow, she says, falls just to cover the trail of wolves on their
    way to the monastery where the moon never enters
it's so afraid of being mistaken for a host.

EARLY CHILDHOOD

for Alain Bosquet

A star
is the invention of a flame
The whim of a spark
the opinion of a lamp longing for eternity
a clandestine movement of God revealed by dictionaries.

My mother would lose herself in the puffing movements of her
    broom
battling the sand which she called desert
the dampness she called crumbled water
swamp

remote from the world her sweeper's hands
exhumed invisible corpses
pursued the least foundering of the wind
the slightest stain of darkness
she swept with so much self-abnegation
and burst out laughing in the worst storm
for fear of appearing ill-tempered

Mother you were so modest
you took no credit for the wind which blew just for your arms as
    they swept.

We were taught to mistrust voices which burst through the snow
      on a fixed date
and spoke to us from left to right
as if we came from the dark side of the earth
the underside of the alphabet

as if our walls had to shelter the outside world
defend the interests of the cold
protect the bare space of a person clothed in saltpeter

Unrecognizable, the seasons' faces pressed against our windows
They said they were held captive by our mirrors
spectators of our dumb-show

We threw them our old clothes
we gave them the leftovers of our evaporated meals

Everything was only style and pretense
the house was trompe l'oeil
its beams reflected street-lamps
and the chestnut tree repeated the same text confronting the wind
that dolphin, that glass-blower
Impression of decline which suited our mother's pallid linens
our father's inflamed speeches as he conversed with God through
      the skylight

Theater of delusion and false enthusiasm
only the pain of the Crucified One was real
as he came down from the wall at specified times
leaving on the plaster the indelible mark of his tortured arms.

for May Ménassa

We had explained our despair to the thorn bush and the juniper
our only cousins in that foreign language
we had cried on the shoulder of the pomegranate tree which bled
    on our doorstep every month

We had asked for an audience with the forest
and provided the testimony of two blackbirds who had seen us
    write the word "goat" in both directions
we had vanquished the alphabet

Our shoemaker spoke Sanskrit
the priest and the stream spoke Latin

We were blamed for our ignorance of ornithology
although we knew every star's name, and its precise punctuation
    on the sky's page.

Our cries, she used to say
would scratch the moon's windowpanes
and scrape the corners of tombstones which milked the moon

My mother set the long slope of her back against us
to interrogate the walls' dampness
decipher saltpeter's crumbling alphabet
translate the symbols carved on the underside of the city
which she only knew in profile
since she never ventured further than her shopping-bag
rarely crossing the uncertain borders of her lamp
City which sent us its rejected rains
and sometimes a wheezy snow which hooked its flakes into the
        pomegranate tree's ears

The planet must be cleaned up
God must be cleaned up!
my mother cried, tying her apron.

I write Mother
and an old woman rises in the uncertainty of evening
slips into a wedding dress
stands on tiptoe on her windowsill
calls out to the hostile city
addresses the haughty tribe of streetlights
bares her chest to the clocks
shows them the precise site of her sorrow
disrobes gently for fear of creasing her wrinkles
and unsettling the air

My mother had her own way of undressing
as one would strip the medals from a disgraced general

A cold odor is in my mother's pockets
and three pebbles to break summer's windows
my mother's dress has drunk all November's snow
dead birds' cries have ripped holes in her hem

She chases them from her unconscious arms
insults them with the muteness of words
and the absence of echoes
within her walls knocked over
from within

It sometimes happens that despite the air's vigilance my mother
    gets up
arms herself with a spade
turns over great shovelfuls of earth which cover her
arousing the anger of taciturn neighbors who've turned their backs
    on the clocks

and broken off all correspondence with the grass
her chilled puffing and panting break through the soil down to that
    room
where, for lack of sun, she makes her knees shine and her tears
    sparkle.

My mother who recalled a blurred-over death
said that the light was stubborn
and embarrassed the crowd which turned its back on her

on the dim landing where voices bustled
her body plunged in grief separated itself from the bedding
the creaking of the floorboards revealed the movements of floor-
    buffing angels
tedious preparations for someone who barked as she chased her
    own breath
a sympathetic hand flung a stone at her across a sob

My mother had paired her basil with the forest oak
inviting it Easter after Easter to share the lamb's grass and bleating
and to verify against its height if we had grown along with the
    lamp
which pushed the sun back behind the hedges
when maternal fingers tucked up a lock of wavy hair

The shutters looked regretful
when my mother read the cards for the night
the king of hearts atop the ten of diamonds
meant moving
the jack of clubs who was afraid of dying
kept his distance from the queen of spades
whom he knew only by her profile

The house was on the edge of the road as if on the edge of tears
its windows ready to burst into sobs.

Tired of drying a dead man's muddy tears under glass
she turned toward her garden
stanched the sweat of the pomegranate tree
cleaned up the lime tree's droppings

The evening which blued her doorway delivered her up to the
    wrath of nettles
which reclaimed their share of her compassion and shade
and the protection of a wall monopolized by ivy which left on its
    plaster
the indelible mark of its pistil

In her dreams my mother made stacks
of houses without walls
of words without syllables
of dead stars which only shone for her sleep
keeping the gardens for insomniac nights
when it was imperative to convene the nightingales
to tell them her dream which they'd pass down from father to son

My mother opened her wardrobe to dead leaves which traveled far
    from their branches
folding them into the weave of her sheets
hems and veins dressed in the same darknesses
The key made a weird sound when a ragged forest appeared at the
    door
to claim its share of the linens' shade
leaving its soil-mark of shame on our doorstep.

Give me a star to light my lamp
some salt to preserve the shutters' tears
some oil to soothe the doors' wounds
two arms to bury the fear-frozen bread

Your voice, mother, addressing God through the skylight
made the soil bite the pomegranate tree

My mother wandered so far in her dreams
that we found her bed empty even of
sheets which she took with her to those lands trod by her sleeping
     feet
where she lost her bracelets and her soul
all rediscovered under her pillow with the invisible guidebook of
     her sleep

My mother who would lose herself in the fire
gave our house over to the affliction of winter
and the shadow of the streetlight playing sextant

We had to look for her in the earth where she'd dug her den
cry out her name among the stones
frighten our own voices and the echo which had seen my mother
     and the fire…pass by.

She used to throw her old crockery at the moon
which mends chipped plates
darns wedding sheets
and sorts lamplight-yellowed snapshots by degrees of sadness

The whole universe shared my mother's household chores
contrary winds blew into her bureau drawers
bargained between her shutters
and swept towards town the dream-crumbs she nibbled in her
    sleep

Negligent mother
clouds of a dubious whiteness dried out on your clothesline
provoking the nightingales' sarcasm and saddening the sun
you reported them missing to the police when the wind carried
    them out of the valley
called the wind a thief of sheets and cattle
then withdrew your complaint when the clouds came home to you,
    fog kneeling on your doorstep.

The salt my mother tossed into her oven
unleashed flame-tongues
and stretched our bodies as far
as Lake Baïkal
the banks of the Euphrates
and the Amazon

We had brought back blue toucans in our hair
breadfruit trees between our teeth
we had eaten acid fruit which made the table screw up its face
chewed red grass which gave the walls hallucinations

In my mother's oven the rumor-bearing winds set on each other
the Amazon's rivers immolated themselves in the Atlantic
the bells of Tibet strangled in their own ropes

we listened to all their grievances
we sympathized.

for Henriette Joël

Huddled between walls, we would talk
about the ones who lived out on the hill
with their lamps in a season of repeated snows
crying out their names when fires spread which could only be seen
     from the clouds
chasing whole families of yellow broom
The bleating of the year's dead goats was sour
the smoke of their quarrels and their brides' laundry were bitter
Our dreams about their women were shut tight
and the hearth was shut where reveries' white water kept boiling
our bread-boxes overflowed with silent bread

The world rocked itself back and forth when they stamped out
     their last fire
the wind which swept their doorstep was crying.

We knew an alphabet of the fields
which lost its breath going uphill
and zigzagged like a Mongolian train
Our alphabet spoke Aramaic so it could converse with the
      country's sun

We were crammed in between A and Z
We weren't on good terms with the accents
and we weren't gifted at gathering commas beneath the lines

All the same, we had come to an agreement with their birds
opened our doors to their winds which couldn't line up two words
and had to make do with crying within our walls.

for Norma Bosquet

66

We stole kisses from the holy pictures
hasty embraces from the cherry tree
plumes from the fog seated on our doorstep

We were highwaymen in the dry season
petty thieves in the rainy season when rivers climbed into our
    bedrooms
we had committed numerous pilferings with angel accomplices
stolen sticks of incense from the cypress
chalk from the dawn
tears from the cemetery walls

We were grandiloquent fabulists
we uprooted minutes from the clock
and recited our ages backwards.

All logic's order melted with the roof
we applauded the rain falling between our walls
fervently mended rips in the spider-webs

We were irreverent
fetishists
my mother read the cards for mockingbirds
my father slapped the sand
slapped God
when the clouds bled
on the bent back of the sky

Our salvation came from nature
we would trap the rednesses of autumn
the destitution of winter
we would end up in tendrils
in bundles of firewood
to affront the brief rage of the conifers.

Clouds played no part in this story
their shadows on the roofs were not necessary for the unities of
    time and place
they served as simple landmarks for whoever taught algebra to the
    nightingales

The village was so spindly
you could reach it by leaning a ladder against a patch of sky

The poplar tree was spindly too
will it be the same translated into French
will it answer to a name that perhaps won't suit its branches used
    to conversing with an Arab wind which postponed autumn for
    a week
so they could finish inventorying their leaves.

Don't turn the pages backwards
said my mother
reversed words get dizzy
disrupted ink curdles like spoiled milk

The books we browsed in came from the forest which watched us
    read
from the peeled bark's shriek which continued under the pages'
    skin
We read in the darkness of August
when the galaxy disposed of its excess stars
when, without margins, night stretched itself out until night.

The bedroom curtains darkened themselves
to veil the nakedness of the one I call my mother
The sheets were cold not the panting of the man
who labored in that closed-in space and not the cry which
        splattered the snow of her belly
smashing its red water
tethering my mother to that house where she remembers.

We had only our heads and all that noise inside them
we had re-routed our origins by threading our names on
     backwards
led the beds into error by sleeping head-to-foot with our shadows

We were absent-minded adversaries
the cocks refereed our vowel-matches
the clocks were responsible for our forgetfulness

Bag of magpies!
Bag of magpies! cried the weather-vanes through our insomnia

Bagamaga mocked the illiterate echo.

No use re-soling our books
our hands will grow into clogs
and our feet into toucan wings

We limped from always walking under the lines
squinted from making faces at the alphabet

Nature isn't fond of unleashed heartless children
who count stars on their bare fingers

We ran alongside walls which burst out laughing
and had long chats with the shutters we'd importuned

Still, a plane tree several moons old
explained that what shone in the sky were our scattered souls.

Tomorrow it will be winter, said my mother
her hands snatching up children and dead leaves left on her
      doorstep
to shelter them between the fruit bowl and the lamp

Time had turned itself upside down like an hourglass
we knew the exact weight of clouds on our eyelids
the air's precise content of tears and cries
how many minutes it took for the light to panic

No one was fooled by the season's maneuvers
we watched out for migrant birds
urged them to trample the sky which had broken its promises
and to announce with enraged wings below the horizon how
      they'd been done wrong.

A prisoner in the close circle of her lamp
she spoke to us of prairies paved by the moon
of hate-filled winds which stabbed each other beneath her
     windows
tousled the weather-cocks' plumage
tore an equidistant tolling from the bells
dived into the olive tree
shouted from its branches
carried on their battle among its leaves
bloodying the wool of low-hanging clouds with their cries

My mother complained of insomnia
caused by angels chattering beneath her windows
they were arguing which path to take to Ursa Major
who was having her annual rummage sale of stars bought by dark
     countries
which would use them for streetlights.

Men and storks go their way
only the cherry tree stays put
repeated my mother

We ate the cherry-stones
and threw the flesh straight up at the evening star
making a wish to be reborn as cherry trees
with a natal stream
and names which could be read in darkness
so that we could squat at the road's edge
and talk until dawn with the stones.

It was the first of November
we unpacked our clothes to see if we'd grown with the streetlights
my brother the seminarian was as tall as his chasuble
my eldest sister gave her skirts to the laurel
my mother buried her bleeding laundry beneath the sycamore
squatted at its feet
rolled back its bark
drank its milk
soiling her blouse and the sapwood's wan belly

A day stuffed with incense and regrets
the fortunate ones who picnicked on the grass
hung their haloes on the tombstones.

We offered the city the rectitude of our walls
the tacit agreement of our skylights
the round monotony of our small parks
begging it to spare the cemetery
its porous earth distills snowflakes drop by deafening drop
the sound crosses the earth on a single note
drowns hearts stuck in the sand
song of dark water in the darkness of lamps held up by darkened
    sleepers.

She drove away her windows
stripped her shutters bare
invited the moon into her bed
warmed it between her thighs
brought down its milk

Laundry stained with black kisses dried on her roof
and disturbed the mourning doves
the down in the walls' niches came from the belly
of a woman who clutched the air so she wouldn't drop into its cry

My mother disliked the snow which spied on her through the
	windows
she preferred the fog whose cotton she pulled out
to wipe her mouth which had wept red in the pillow's hollows.

Years later
we have yet to explain the lime tree's muteness
and the well's determination to kill

We were all responsible for the day's rapid decline
for the cry which divided the waters
scattering children and larks

The little girl who didn't know how to hang on to the air
was a liquid sketch on the paving-stones
her knees useless pebbles
her yellow dress a stain of shame and sun

In the house open to compassion
the wind seated in front of the fireplace
received condolences and distributed tears.

for May Ménassa

Enraged at not being able to catch us
the winds attacked our houses
which they thrust into the ground
blinding the windowpanes

We attributed the moon's appearance in our mirrors to an optical
        illusion
maligned it in its presence

The country was so narrow at that time
the dead and the living slept five in a bed with their troubles
it was God's business to blush at such a situation, not the rose's,
victim of the lustful sun which infiltrated its pistil
tearing apart the fused petals at its heart.

It had always been expected that we would inherit the patch of
    blue land
which hung above our houses
we had planned how we'd gather the rains
how we'd divide the light
and transfer the moon to a less exposed spot

We learned to spell the name of God in darkness
to knead it with the salt of our lips
to melt it in edible prayers
in songs
in smoke
not knowing that if we just blew out his lamp we could reach his
    acre of ether and eternity.

She drowned all the cats
and all the vowels
drew a mirror on her wall
the swallows that crossed it left their black cries on it
and the sun left its roundness

She wrung out the cats and the vowels
seated them on chairs
erased her mirror
crawled under the furniture in search of the crumbled alphabet.

My mother accused the poet who'd been dead for a century
of stirring her voice into his notebooks
of multiplying the winds in her corners
of torturing the snow of her belly
and swinging in violent arcs from her nut-tree's one branch
The graveyard watchman bit the walls till they bled
so as not to answer the woman who swore at the dead man with
    her mouth to the earth
and refused him at night in her wide bed
for fear of conceiving a child come on foot from the next world.

They photographed the month of April naked
soiled the almond tree's underwear
pressed the poppy's black heart between two stones

We associated with them only at solstices
when the days shortened their skirts up to dusk
and fireflies copulated in lamps

We lost sight of them after the scandal that tarnished the night
suspected of milking the moon to sell its cream to rich galaxies.

They no longer prostrated themselves between stopped clocks
no longer guessed at the invisible number
they had lost confidence in the four-leaf clover
and the stork had beguiled their children away from the opaque
     side of the air

They no longer followed the Milky Way home
or turned off the road after the North Star
their tears came from the willow
and their milk from jasmine whose teats they'd pull at dusk

They no longer hunted archangels
or sympathized with hollyhocks
exposed to the moon, their dead crumbled in silence
until their skeletons had completely evaporated.

The storks came home empty-handed
they'd have to go past Manchuria to find the children
on the knees of the fifth season
whose name is brambles and felicity

At that time, the earth was pregnant with the North Star
winds hounded her from east to west
while galaxies barked

The child who'd be born would limp from the heart
said my mother
as she mended Cassiopeia's chair.

They colonized the country at nightfall
beat back the trees with rifle-butts
made the fire flee

Our smoke brought tears to their vowels' eyes
their consonants caught fire at the mere sight of a match
We had smoked their green tongue with cannabis
kneaded their white tongue in our bread-boxes
laid their red tongue down in our beds
drowned the blue one in our ink

Their chilly tongue was hung in our attics when the rivers flooded
shaken out over the railings to scatter the last crumbs of silence
dried on our rooftops when it rained in their alphabet.

How could we believe the promises of a minor planet
which works off the books for a galaxy
banished to the suburbs of the universe?

We watched all night to see it pass by
brandishing tracts protesting our innocence in the conspiracy
     which broke up the universe
lit it with a sun which turned for its own pleasure
and took a census of the stars every evening
for fear of playing before an empty world.

From our balconies, we watched the illness progress, attacking
    the old comets
our compassion going towards those which had left the populated
    areas and withdrawn to an outlying part of the sky
We watched them reel in the darkness
exhaust themselves climbing
stagger with their lanterns extinguished
we blew them out to put an end to their suffering
finished them off with a rifle-shot
then buried them in a hole in the air.

How could we walk along the girders of a syntax which languages
    push from beach to beach turning the letters into landmarks
    which warn of quicksand?
Numerous, we were on our guard against words' irascibility and
    their stubborn insistence on linking themselves together to
    cordon off the way to the unsayable
from the wind which had only one gesture of protest: creating
    repetitive waves and that noise of the world's beginning, that
    one language spoken by the four horizons
which surround the square of earth spattered by water.

Sorrowful season
the rain on the wharf was torturing a ship
and the dead scattered to the four corners of their bodies were
    mended by women's hands

Sometimes,
at the crossroads of two abandoned cities, doors we'd thought long
    drowned sprang up and banged all night beneath the bog
Nothing predicted such rejection coming from a submissive earth
    which chewed bones and stones indiscriminately
No one expected to see these bloodless boards reclaim their now-
    groundless thresholds.

We made fires which licked the clouds' chasubles
and the Creator's footsoles

It was forbidden to play on the swings on Midsummer's Eve
the bonfires' smoke carried children higher than the angels
up where the universe is so deaf that it's useless to call out to it

At that time we coveted objects without contours
petrified water or mirrors we could penetrate with our flashlights

We were the traces of invisible bodies
the marks of ancient tracks dissolved in the air's memory.

We had been placed on the earth
with glass tears attached to our eyelashes
and arms crossed on a faded odor

We had been taught not to count the stars
for fear of angering Hecuba who barks at the sky's iron gates
our dead had been taught not to move facing the sun
for fear of blurring the image of God.

Escaped from a shipwreck on the high lands
we settled down on an arable sea
with inert waves
and seagulls sculpted from salt

Vertical winds erected our walls
the hulls of grounded boats became our beds

We went aboard behind our eyelids
with the brotherhood of algae
rooted to a sleep in which only dreams circulated freely

And sometimes
through the fog of blood
came other survivors other sleepers
it became urgent to move out of that ocean
traveling away in nothing but our voices
leaving behind us absent houses and keys which only knew how to
    grumble in the doors.

The confusion of a railway car astray on the tracks
raised smoke which leaned heavily on our windows
lingered over our ancestors lined up at posthumous attention
their yellowed lips flying off in the squall like dead leaves
their chilly lips cautiously chewing the smoke
before returning it to the train station which remembered.

The dead woman stayed cool beneath the maple tree
her back turned toward the house which had not kept her
her outmoded dress embarrassed the sparrows
her tangled hair would re-cane the chairs hung from the branches
tired angels stopped there
long enough to ascertain if the woman had come that far with the
     sun.

The cycle of sorrow ends beneath the sole of the archangel
who has lost a wing
and who looks at his hands in desolation
the dead with their lightweight linens have burrowed under the
    tombstones
since all the fervent inscriptions turned to ice.

One must lift the dawn up to see the poet seated atop the
    landscape
he is neither detractor nor eulogist
but pale because he was conceived in a time of heavy snow
with a round face
because his mother sat down on the moon to take a pebble from
    her shoe.

Here there was once a country
fire withdrew from women's fingers
bread deserted the ploughed furrows
and the cold devoured all children who wore daffodils on their
    shoulders

Here there was once a wall
which reproduced itself in prosperous times
became rectangle square but never circle
so as not to humiliate the fountains
which held the rights to day's roundness

Here there was once a hunter
who knocked down his house to go into the forest
and verify that his shots pierced the eardrums of the rocks

Here there was once a pebble
which turned into a gravestone at the mere sight of a passer-by

Here there was once an infinitely white night
an infinitely black tree
which pulled its bark up to its chin
when noon lengthened shadows down to the ravine

Here there was once the echo of another echo
and the horns of great cattle which melted when even a wing
    passed overhead.

ACKNOWLEDGMENTS

Grateful acknowledgment is given to the editors of the journals in which these poems originally appeared: *Ambit* (U.K.), *Banipal: a Journal of Modern Arab Literature* (U.K.), *Connect*, *FIELD*, *Luna*, *Metre* (Ireland), *Shenandoah*, and *Verse*. The poems from "Early Childhood" beginning "She used to throw her old crockery…," "No use re-soling our books," and "We made fires which licked the clouds' chasubles" first appeared in *Poetry*.

ABOUT THE AUTHOR AND TRANSLATOR

Vénus Khoury-Ghata is a Lebanese poet and novelist, resident in France since 1973. She has published many collections of poems and novels, including *Anthologie personnelle*, new and selected poems (1997), and *Elle dit,* her most recent collection (1999). Her awards include the Prix Mallarmé, the Prix Apollinaire, and the Grand Prix de la Société des gens de lettres. Her work has been translated into Italian, Russian, Dutch, German, and Arabic; Marilyn Hacker's translations of her poems have appeared in periodicals in the United States, England, and Ireland.

Marilyn Hacker is the author of nine books of poetry, including the verse novel *Love, Death and the Changing of the Seasons* and her most recent collection, *Squares and Courtyards* (2000). *A Long-Gone Sun*, her translation of Claire Malroux's *Soleil de Jadis,* was published in 2000. Her awards include the National Book Award, two Lambda Literary Awards, and the Lenore Marshall Award. Former editor of *The Kenyon Review*, she lives in New York and Paris, and is director of the M.A. program in English literature and creative writing at the City College of New York.